Hearing His Voice with Grace

Susan Leffler

His voice speaks love.

His voice brings peace.

His voice gives joy.

Listen.

His voice speaks truth.

His voice brings understanding.

His voice gives guidance.

Listen.

Hear Him.

It's God!

Hi, my name is Grace and this is my puppy Oscar.
I want to talk to you about hearing God's voice.

God can speak to you in many different ways.
He could speak to you in a powerful thunderous voice.

The Lord thundered from heaven, and the Most High uttered His voice.
Psalm 18:13

God can speak to you by giving you a feeling or just
a knowing that this is what you should or shouldn't do.

LEFT
RIGHT
STRAIGHT +
NARROW PATH

"I feel like GOD is leading me this way."

God also speaks to you through His words in the Bible.

...give attention to my words; incline your ear to my sayings. Do not let them depart from your eyes; keep them in the midst of your heart; for they are life to those who find them and health to all their flesh.

Prov 4:20-22

PSALM 23:1

The Lord is my shepherd;

God will speak to you in dreams and visions.

At Gibeon the Lord appeared to Solomon in a dream by night;
and God said, "Ask! What shall I give you?"

1 Kings 3:5

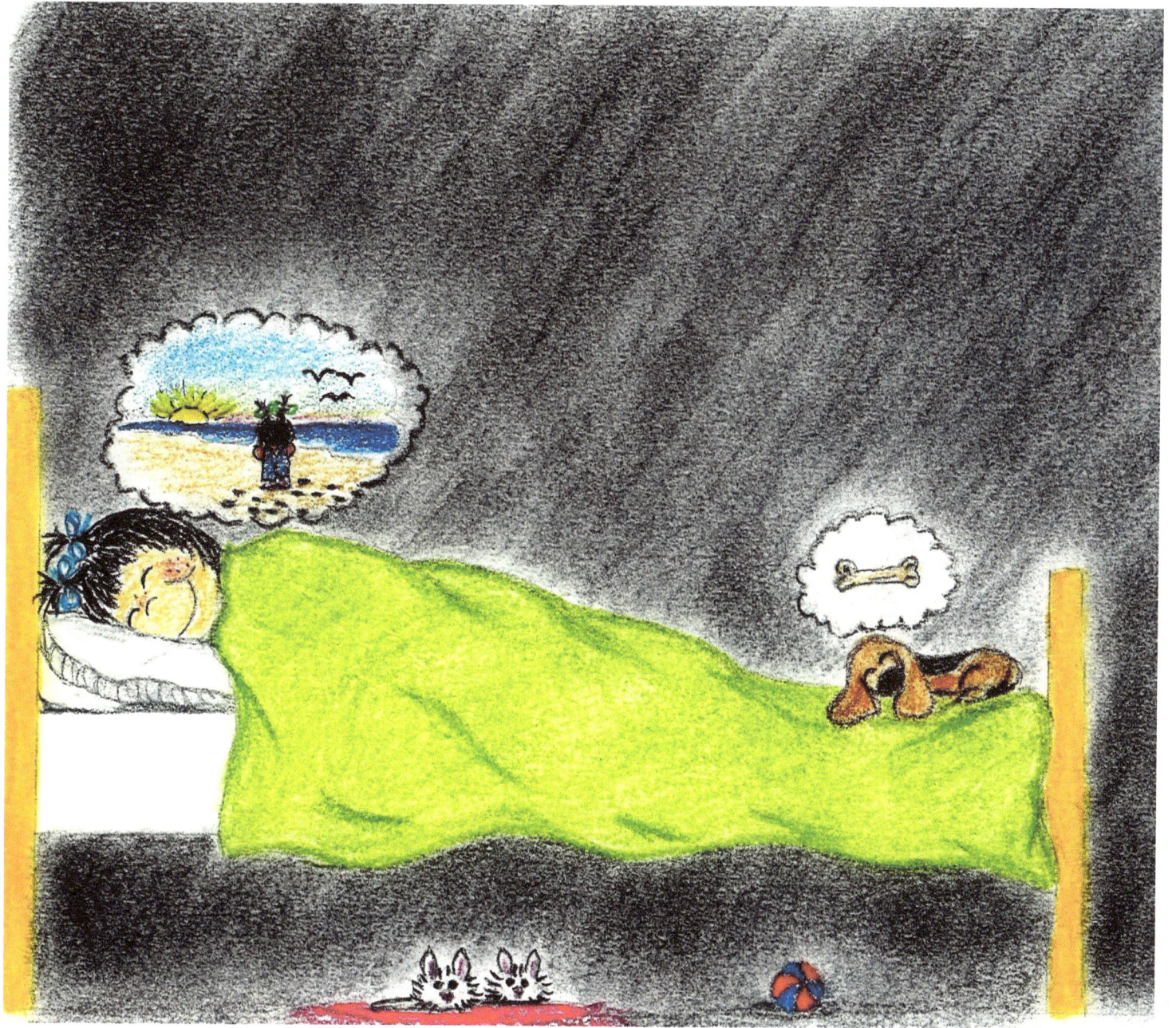

But God really likes to speak to you in a still small voice.

...and after the earthquake a fire, but the Lord was not in the fire;
and after the fire a still small voice.

1 Kings 19:12

Long ago God would speak to men like Moses and the prophets. The prophet would then tell the people what God said and what God wanted them to do.

…God called to him from the midst of the bush and said, "Moses, Moses…"
And Moses hid his face for he was afraid to look upon God. And God said to Moses,
"I AM WHO I AM." And He said, "This you shall say to the children of Israel,
'I AM has sent me to you."

Ex 3:4, 6, 14

But when Jesus came, He taught that each and every one of us can hear from Father God.

"Father, glorify Your name." Then a voice came from heaven, saying, "I have both glorified it and will glorify it again." Therefore the people who stood by and heard it said that it had thundered. Others said, "An angel has spoken to Him." Jesus answered and said, "This voice did not come because of Me, but for your sake."

John 12:28-30

Jesus would often go off by himself and pray to Father God. I would imagine He asked Father God for guidance and what He should say to the people. Jesus said...

"For I have not spoken on My own authority; but the Father who sent Me gave Me a command, what I should say and what I should speak. And I know that His command is everlasting life. Therefore, whatever I speak, just as the Father has told Me, so I speak."

John 12:49-50

...Jesus came up immediately from the water; and behold, the heavens were opened to Him, and He saw the Spirit of God descending like a dove and alighting upon Him. And suddenly a voice came from heaven, saying, "This is My beloved Son, in whom I am well pleased."

Matt 3:16-17

Jesus told us that the sheep know their shepherds voice.
That is because a shepherd watches over his sheep
protecting them, leading them and guiding them
with his voice. He is with them all the time.

God is with us all the time.

And when he brings out his own sheep, he goes before them: and the sheep follow
him, for they know his voice. I am the good shepherd; and I know My sheep,
and am known by My own.

John 10:4, 14

If you sit quietly and listen, you can hear God's voice.
Sometimes it is the first thought that pops into your head.

God's voice will instruct you and teach you and lead you
into your destiny that He has for you.

God will always say and tell you good things. You will always
feel love and peace from God's voice. That is how you know
it is God speaking. God wants the best for you.

Oscar knows my voice. I talk to Oscar all the time.
I talk to Oscar when I feed him, when I take him for a walk
and when we play and have fun. Oscar knows I always have
good things for him so he always comes when I call him.

God always has good things for you too!
He is with you all the time. He will never leave you.
Nothing can separate you from God's love.

For I know the thoughts that I think toward you, says the Lord, thoughts of peace
and not of evil, to give you a future and a hope.

Jer 29:11

God is good all the time. He never changes.
God likes to have fun with us. Sometimes my friends
and I like to play Holy Spirit hide-n-seek.

I count to ten and my friends all hide. Then I ask God,
"Where are they hiding Papa?" And if I listen closely, I will
hear God's still small voice say, "Look behind the tree."

Jesus Christ is the same yesterday, today and forever.

Heb 13:8

It is God's desire that you hear His voice.
He is speaking to you all the time. God's voice will always
bring you peace and make you feel happy.

God's voice would never, ever tell you to do something wrong
or make you feel bad. God loves you and will always
lead you into doing the right things.

God has big plans for each and every one of us.
But it is up to you to hear and obey His voice
so you can step into the life He has destined for you.

God is waiting for you to talk to Him. He hears all of your
prayers. God is a good listener!

Then you will call upon Me and go and pray to Me, and I will listen to you.
Jer 29:12

Just imagine yourself sitting on Papa God's lap and telling Him all about the desires of your heart and your secrets.

You can ask Him anything.
God wants to share His heart with you too.

One time I was sitting and thinking about God and all of a sudden I heard the word, "ketchup."

I said, "Papa, was that you?
Why would you give me the word ketchup?"
He said, "I just wanted to see if you were listening."

I smiled and said, "I love you Papa."

God said, "I love you too Gracie."

Now this is the confidence that we have in Him, that if we ask anything according to His will, He hears us.

1 John 5:14

Accepting Jesus

To know love is to know Jesus. And to know Jesus is to know God the Father, because God is love.

If you want to know Jesus and the Father's love, ask Him into your life. He will show you and tell you all about His love for you, just like He did with me.

Just say;

"Jesus, I believe in my heart you are the Son of God and that you are my Lord and Savior. I ask you into my life and I receive my salvation now. Thank you Jesus for saving me."

Receive the Holy Spirit

If you just said that prayer and accepted Jesus into your life,
or if Jesus is already part of your life, then God the Father
wants to give you His Holy Spirit.

The Holy Spirit will live in you and will guide you
and teach you in the way of the Father.
All you have to do is ask, believe and receive.

Just say;

"Father, I ask for your power and your guidance to live this
new life you have for me. Please fill me with your Holy Spirit.
I receive Him right now. Thank you for baptizing me
with your Holy Spirit."

Gracie's Prayer

Thank you Father for your love and grace.

You make me smile bigger than my face.

Let me hear your voice throughout the day

And dreams and visions at night I pray.

Thank you God, Father of lights,

I love you and bless you and say goodnight!

www.ingramcontent.com/pod-product-compliance
Lightning Source LLC
Chambersburg PA
CBHW042121040426

42449CB00003B/130